TOUCHING AND FEELING

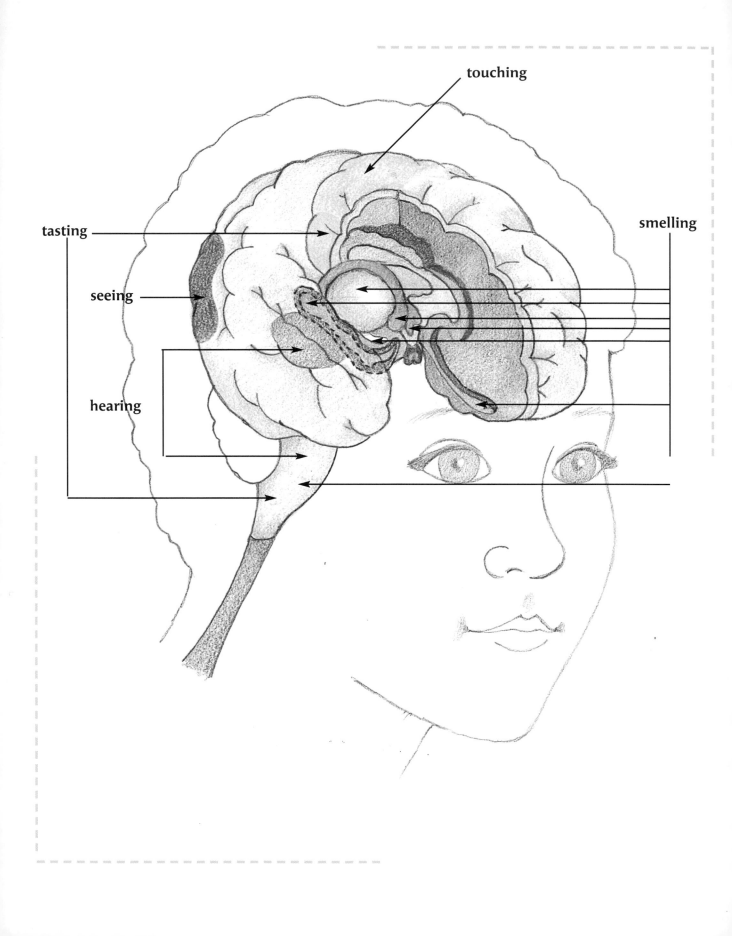

touching

smelling

tasting

seeing

hearing

Touching AND Feeling

Dr. Alvin Silverstein, Virginia Silverstein, and Laura Silverstein Nunn

SENSES AND SENSORS
Twenty-First Century Books
Brookfield, Connecticut

Cover illustration by Anne Canevari Green

Photographs courtesy of SuperStock: pp. 8, 15; PhotoEdit: pp. 10 (© David Young-Wolff), 27 (© Spencer Grant), 29 (© Tony Freeman), 43 (© Myrleen Ferguson), 44 (© Myrleen Ferguson), 46 (© Jeff Greenberg), 47 (© Michael Newman); Animals Animals: pp. 12 (© Robert Maier), 36 (© O.S.F.), 37 (© Leen Van Der Slik), 38 (© S. Morris, O.S.F.), 41 (© Robert Maier); Peter Arnold, Inc.: p. 14 (© Alex Grey); Archive Photos: p. 19; Photo Researchers, Inc.: pp. 23 (© Cristina Pedrazzini/SPL), 50 (© James King-Holmes/SPL), 52 (© Mauro Fermariello/SPL), 55 (© Sam Ogden/SPL); Visuals Unlimited, Inc.: pp. 35 (© M. Abbey), 39 (© David Sieren); Phototake: p. 54 (© Richard T. Nowitz)

Illustrations by Anne Canevari Green

Library of Congress Cataloging-in-Publication Data
Silverstein, Alvin
Touching and feeling / Alvin Silverstein, Virginia Silverstein and Laura Silverstein Nunn.
p. cm. — (Senses and sensors)
Includes index.
ISBN 0-7613-1668-X (lib. bdg.)
1. Touch—Juvenile literature. [1. Touch. 2. Senses and sensation.] I. Silverstein, Virginia B. II. Nunn, Laura Silverstein. III. Title. IV. Series.
QP451 .S49 2001 612.8'8—dc21
2001018093

Published by Twenty-First Century Books
A Division of The Millbrook Press, Inc.
2 Old New Milford Road
Brookfield, Connecticut 06804
www.millbrookpress.com

CONTENTS

TOUCHING AND FEELING

The sense of touch is very important in helping us learn about the elements that surround us. Most of the time we are not even aware of the many pleasant and unpleasant sensations that affect our daily experiences.

1 KEEPING IN TOUCH WITH THE WORLD

Everything we know about the world comes through our five senses—seeing, hearing, smelling, tasting, and touching. When you eat an apple, you may be aware of many things: its bright red color, the crunchy sound as you bite into it, its sweet smell, and the taste that floods your mouth as you bite and chew. You might not be so aware of some other sensations that you are receiving at the same time: the smoothness of the apple's skin and its firm, rounded shape; the feel of it in your mouth as you bite off a crunchy piece and chew it into a soft mush. Even if you were blindfolded and your nose were stopped up with a cold, you could still easily tell the difference between a bite of apple and a spoonful of applesauce or a sip of apple juice—just by the way they feel.

Touching and feeling are very important parts of our lives. We greet friends and family with a hug and kiss. Football players often give each other a hug after winning a big game. A cool shower feels great on a hot day, and so does a warm sweater when it is chilly outside.

Some feelings are not so pleasant—the pain when you scrape your knee after falling off a bike, for example. What about that scary feeling you get when you are about to take a test or give a speech?

DID YOU KNOW?

The organs for our other four senses—seeing, hearing, smelling, and tasting—are all located in the head. Our main organ of touch, however, is the skin, which covers the whole surface of the body.

The sense of touch reinforces the perception that we are in direct contact with the world around us.

THE MEANINGS OF FEELINGS

We use the word "feeling" to describe a number of different things. It can refer to using our sense of touch—feeling the smoothness of a silk shirt or the hard edge of a table. We also use "feeling" for sensations that come from inside us: the hungry feeling you get when you haven't eaten for a while; the queasy feeling after you eat something that didn't agree with you; the "warm feeling" you get when someone tells you that you did a good job. These inner feelings are usually linked with something our bodies need, such as food or water; warnings that something is wrong; or emotional reactions to situations.

In this book, we will discuss touching and feeling. Whether you are pricking your finger on a thorny rose, hugging a friend, or dipping your toes in an icy swimming pool, you are receiving impressions of the world. The sense of touch can even give you information about imaginary worlds. Working the joystick while you play a video game, for example, you can feel the shaking of the steering wheel as you steer a race car. We are more conscious of the messages from our eyes and ears, perhaps, but touch is often the main sense that helps us to feel involved, that makes an experience truly "real."

All living organisms—humans, animals, and even plants—have senses. They gather information about the world through specialized structures called **sensors**. These sensors detect various types of energy and send information about them to the brain to be translated into meaningful messages. Many of our touch, or **tactile**, sensors are located on the outside of the body—the skin—in the part of us that is in direct contact with the world.

Some animals rely on their tactile senses far more than we do. Many insects use the touch-sensitive hairs on their antennae, wings, legs, and body to detect danger in the air and on the water. The hairs can pick up the vibrations of approaching predators.

A cat uses its whiskers to detect vibrations from the movements of its prey, or to "feel" its way through the dark and avoid obstacles.

Inventors and researchers have developed machines and electronic devices that imitate or substitute for the touch sensors of living things. These artificial sensors can expand our natural abilities, allowing us to work at a distance or to manipulate objects too tiny to be seen without a microscope, and can make toys and electronic games more entertaining.

2 THE SKIN SENSES

Imagine a day in your life: When you get out of bed and head for the bathroom, you stub your toe on the sneakers you left in the middle of the floor. Ouch! That hurts! You feel chilly as you remove your clothes for your morning shower, but then warm water pouring over your body feels really good. When you get out of the shower, you feel a chill again until you put on your warm, comfortable clothes.

On the way to school, a stone gets caught inside your shoe. You can feel that it is rough and pointy, and it hurts your foot until you remove it. When you see your friends at school, you may greet them with a slap on the back, a high five, or a friendly hug. Throughout the day, your fingers are busy handling all sorts of things—pens, pencils, books, papers, and gym equipment, such as balls, bats, or hockey sticks.

When you get home from school, you grab an orange for a snack. The orange looks round and smooth, but it feels slightly bumpy under your fingertips. As you plop down onto the couch to watch TV, the cushions feel soft and comfortable, helping you to relax after a long, busy day.

Every single day, from the moment we wake up in the morning until we go to bed at night, we are flooded with information about the way things feel. What we think of as our sense of touch actually includes a number of different senses. We perceive all of them through our skin, and each "skin sense" has its own special sense receptors. These skin senses include touch and pressure, pain,

DID YOU KNOW?

An average person's skin has about 15 million tiny nerve endings for transmitting sensations.

13

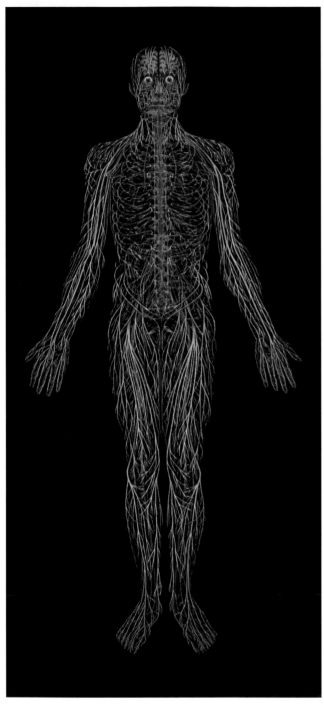

All the information gathered through our sense receptors is carried to our brain from the complex network of nerves that runs throughout our entire body.

warmth, and cold. When the sense receptors are stimulated, they send messages to the brain and spinal cord, which decide whether they are signals for action. For instance, if you cut your finger, nerve endings in the skin send messages to your brain that your finger is being hurt.

THE CENTRAL CONNECTION

The skin sensors are at the ends of a branching network of nerves that reaches out to all parts of the body. These nerves bring sense messages to the brain and spinal cord, which together make up the **central nervous system (CNS)**. The nerves that carry sense messages are called **sensory nerves**.

Another nerve network also branches out from the CNS to the farthest reaches of the body. These nerves are called **motor nerves** because they carry messages from the CNS to the muscles and other organs, and produce actions, many of which are movements. The CNS is the body's central processing station, which interprets sense messages, makes decisions on what actions are needed, and sends out commands to produce these actions.

We don't actually "feel" anything until sense messages are processed in the brain. But some of the messages are so urgent that the time it takes for messages to be sent to the brain and processed there might be too long. The delay might result in the body getting hurt. For instance, you immediately jerk your hand

OUR FIRST REFLEXES

Even a newborn baby has some ready-made reflexes that can help it survive. If a nipple touches its cheek, the baby turns its head to find the nipple and starts to suck on it. If you touch the palm of the baby's hand with your finger, it will immediately grab your finger and hold on so tight that it could even support the weight of its body if you lifted it! This automatic grasping reflex disappears after a few months, but later the baby learns to grab and hold things on purpose.

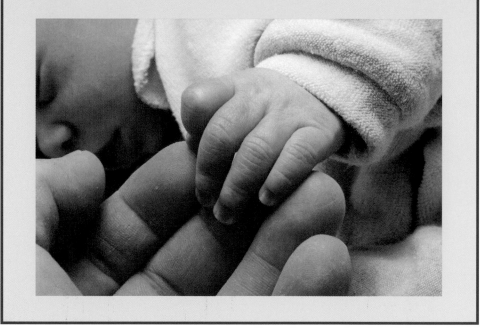

away when you touch a hot stove. If you had to wait until you were aware of the heat and thought about pulling your hand away, you would already be burned. Automatic reactions like this are called **reflexes**. They are handled by the spinal cord. Later (after you are safe) the sense messages may be relayed up to the brain, and you finally realize what happened.

Certain routine actions are also handled by reflexes. When you first learn to tie your shoes, for example, you have to think very hard about each finger movement needed in forming the bow. But

1. The heat triggers a pain receptor in your finger. 2. The pain receptor sends a signal along the sensory neuron to the spinal cord. 3. In the spinal cord, the signal takes a shortcut. 4. The motor neurons activate your muscles to pull your hand away from the pain immediately. 5. By the time the pain signals from your finger arrive at your brain, your hand is already out of danger.

as you practice, it becomes routine—a learned reflex. Your fingers move automatically without your having to think about what they are doing. In fact, if you do think about it—for example, if you are teaching a younger brother or sister—you may feel confused for a moment and have trouble remembering which movement comes after which. The same thing also happens for other learned reflexes such as riding a bicycle or typing on a computer.

3 TOUCH AND PRESSURE

Close your eyes. Have someone place an object in front of you without telling you what it is. Now touch the object with your fingertips. Feel its shape and texture. Your fingers will tell you whether it is rough or smooth, hard or soft, wet or dry or sticky. You can feel how big or small it is, and its general shape. Can you guess the object just by touching it?

Your sense of touch is so sensitive that you can recognize many different things just by the way they feel. You can tell if you are touching a soft stuffed animal, a rough, pointy rock, or the contours of a chair.

TOUCH RECEPTORS

Touch receptors are spread over all parts of the body, but they are not spread evenly. Most of the touch receptors are found in your fingertips, tongue, and lips. On the tip of each of your fingers, for example, there are about five thousand separate touch receptors. In other parts of the body there are far fewer. In the skin of your back, the touch receptors may be as much as 2 inches (5 centimeters) apart. You can test this for yourself. Have someone poke you in the back with one, two, or three fingers and try to guess how many fingers the person used. If the fingers are close together, you will probably think it was only one. But if the fingers are spread far apart, you can feel them individually. Yet if the person does the same thing on the back of your hand (with your eyes closed, so that you don't see how many fingers are being used), you probably will be able to tell easily, even when the fingers are close together.

A Touching Life

Helen Keller, who had become blind and deaf at an early age, had to sharpen her sense of touch so she could become better connected with the world around her. When Helen was a young child, her teacher, Anne Sullivan, taught her how to communicate through touch signaling. Anne would place an object in Helen's hand and spell the word out in Helen's other hand. It wasn't long before Helen learned to connect objects with letters. The first word Helen understood was "water," after feeling the liquid running through her fingers. Helen greatly expanded her vocabulary through her hands-on experience and touch signaling. Helen was also able to perform various tasks by feeling other people's hands to "see" what they were doing. She copied their actions and eventually did jobs herself, such as milking the cows and kneading dough. She even learned to recognize people by feeling their faces or clothes.

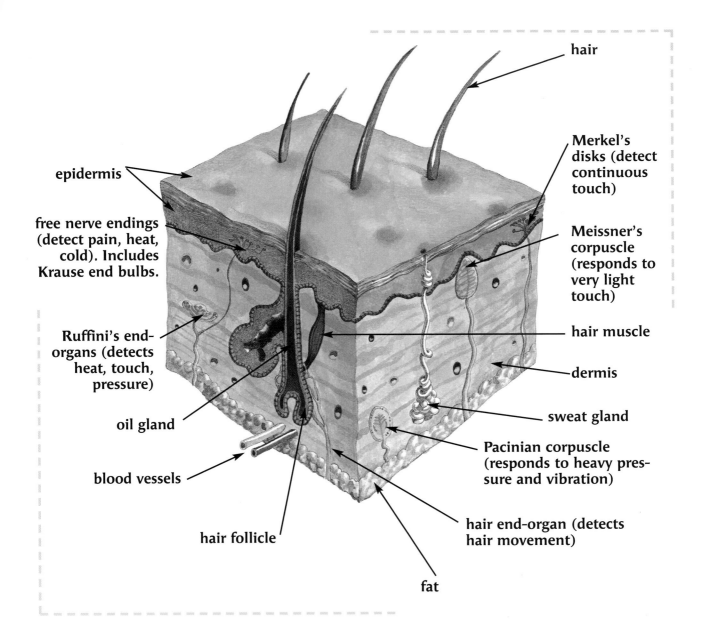

hair

Merkel's disks (detect continuous touch)

Meissner's corpuscle (responds to very light touch)

hair muscle

dermis

sweat gland

Pacinian corpuscle (responds to heavy pressure and vibration)

hair end-organ (detects hair movement)

fat

epidermis

free nerve endings (detect pain, heat, cold). Includes Krause end bulbs.

Ruffini's end-organs (detects heat, touch, pressure)

oil gland

blood vessels

hair follicle

Tactile sensors in the skin provide us with several different kinds of sensations. A touch is usually a light contact of something against the skin. Touch sensors are found near the surface of the skin and can detect the softness of a feather against your cheek. We generally use the word *pressure* to describe a harder touch. Pressure sensors are found deeper in the skin. You use your pressure sensors to feel a book in your hand or the firm floor against your feet when you run or walk. A **vibration** is a series of rapid, repeated touches. We can distinguish even very rapid vibrations—up to 700 cycles per second—from a long, continuous touch. If you place your fingertip lightly against a guitar string after it has just been plucked, you can feel its rapid vibrations. Riding an escalator, you can feel its slower, rumbling vibrations through the soles of your feet.

Various kinds of receptors in the skin help us to tell the difference between a brief, light touch and a hard or heavy pressure; between something moving along our skin (like an ant) and something that stays in contact with us (such as our clothes).

The simplest of all touch receptors are the **free nerve endings**. These nerve endings are stimulated by objects that are in contact with the body surface. They can be found everywhere in the skin and are sensitive to touch as well as pressure. The sensations persist for a long time. You probably know the feeling if you have ever gotten a particle stuck in your eye. It just keeps on bothering you; you never get used to it. The outer covering of your eyeball contains only free nerve endings.

Meissner's corpuscles are sense receptors that respond to very light touch. They are found mostly in the lips, fingertips, and other very sensitive places. These receptors can easily detect the light touch of a crawling spider or ant moving over your skin. In parts of the body that are covered with hairs, light moving touches stimulate a different kind of tactile receptor: the **hair end-organs**. The hair end-organs are actually nerve cells, which are wrapped around the bottom of each hair on the body. They can detect moving objects on the skin surface that brush against the hairs. We do not use this sense as much as many other mammals do.

Merkel's disks are sense receptors that can be found mostly on the tongue and in hairy parts of the body. They are named for their shape; round, flattened disks at the ends of nerve fibers. These receptors detect the continuous touch of objects against the skin.

In the deeper layers of the skin and tissues are **Ruffini's end-organs**. These sense receptors are multibranched nerve endings that respond to pressure and heavy continuous touch stimuli.

Pacinian corpuscles are onion-shaped receptors that can be found all over in the skin, connective tissue near tendons and joints, and various deep tissues. They are very sensitive to pressure and vibrations, even very rapid vibrations.

THE SENSING BRAIN

The various sensors in the skin are only part of our touch sense. Basically, the touch sensors provide raw data. It is up to our brain to interpret the sensory messages for us to feel a touch.

The touch receptors send signals along sensory nerves to the spinal cord. From there, they are then transmitted to a relay station in the brain called the **thalamus**. Finally, they go to the **sensory cortex**, an area of the brain where sensory messages are interpreted, and at last we become aware of the touch.

The sensory cortex is part of the **cerebral cortex**, the thin, outermost covering of the **cerebrum**, the largest part of the brain. The cerebrum is often called the "thinking brain" because it is the region where we think, remember, make decisions, and control the movements of the body. Most of this activity takes place in the cerebral cortex. Here, billions of **neurons** (nerve cells) receive messages from sense receptors and send out messages to control the body's activities.

The cerebrum is separated into left and right halves, or **hemispheres**. The two hemispheres are not completely separated; deep inside the brain, a thick cable of nerve fibers called the **corpus callosum** links the two halves together. Strangely, most of the nerves connecting the cerebrum to the rest of the body cross over to the opposite side as they enter the brain. The brain's crisscross wiring means that movements on the left side of the body are controlled by the right side of the brain, and vice versa; and most of the sense messages that reach each hemisphere come from the opposite side of the body. When you pick up a pencil with your right hand, for example,

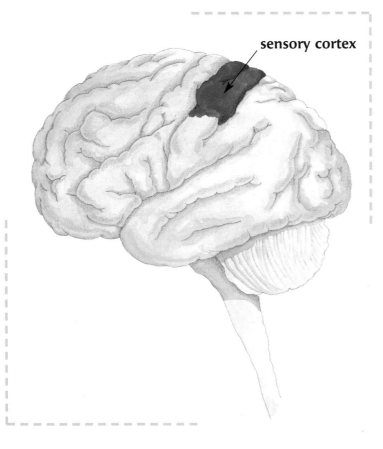

sensory cortex

messages from the skin sensors in your fingers travel up a chain of nerves that ends in a particular area on the *left* side of your cerebral cortex. Another spot on the left side of the cortex sends messages out to your right hand controlling your movements as you lift the pencil and start to write.

Each spot on the surface of the body sends tactile sense messages to a corresponding spot on the cerebral cortex. Scientists have mapped the brain's sense areas by stimulating various spots on the cerebral cortex with electrodes and noting what kind of sensation the person feels. They have found that the processing areas for sense messages from the body are all found on a strip of cortex just behind a groove that runs down each side of the brain, roughly above the ears. These areas are the left and right **sensory strips**, or **somesthetic areas** (from Greek words meaning "body perception"). In front of the same groove on each side lies another key area, the **motor strip**, from which messages are sent out to the various parts of the body to direct movements. You might think that the amounts of space on the sensory and motor strips corresponding to each body part would be roughly proportional to the size of the part. Actually, though, they are proportional to the numbers of sensory or motor nerves that serve each body part. So the regions for the face (especially the lips), the tongue, and the hands are quite large, and those for the body and legs are rather small.

GETTING GOOSEBUMPS

Have you ever seen the tiny hairs on your arms stand straight up just like a cat's fur does when it's scared? When you are cold or scared, your brain sends messages that cause tiny muscles attached to your hair follicles to tighten up. This causes the skin at the base of each hair to swell slightly, creating a bumpy appearance. People call these little bumps "goosebumps" because they make your skin look like that of a plucked goose. They don't do anything useful for humans. But the raised hairs of a scared cat make it look larger and might help to frighten away enemies.

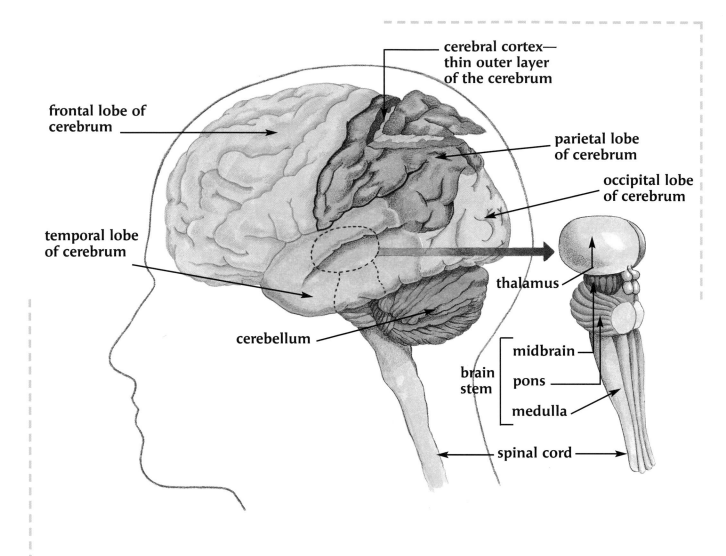

frontal lobe of cerebrum

cerebral cortex— thin outer layer of the cerebrum

parietal lobe of cerebrum

occipital lobe of cerebrum

temporal lobe of cerebrum

thalamus

cerebellum

brain stem

midbrain

pons

medulla

spinal cord

Sometimes the brain has trouble interpreting the sensory messages. This may happen because of the complicated way the network of sensory nerves branches. Messages from different parts of the body may travel up through the same sensory nerve, confusing the brain about which branch they came from. This may cause a **referred sensation**. That's why your nose may itch while the dental hygienist is working on your teeth.

4 FEELING PAIN

We usually think of pain as a bad thing, but actually it can be good for us. Pain acts as a warning that something is wrong, that damage is being done to the body—or may be done, unless immediate action is taken.

PAIN RECEPTORS

Pain receptors are free nerve endings. They can be found in the top layers of the skin as well as in some deeper tissues. Many things can stimulate pain receptors. Hard pressure, extreme heat or cold, certain chemicals, an electric shock—all can give us a sensation of pain. A cut or scrape or anything else that damages tissues will make us feel pain, as long as these tissues have a lot of pain receptors. (Some places inside the body have very few pain receptors or none at all. Surprisingly, the brain itself does not contain any pain receptors.)

HANDLING PAIN

Do you yell and cry when you stub your toe or get a paper cut? Or maybe you handle pain well and are not bothered much by little cuts, bumps, or bruises, although spraining your ankle or breaking your leg

WHERE DOES IT HURT?

Sometimes the brain may be fooled as to the exact origin of pain. For instance, a pain in the heart area (such as a heart attack) may be felt in the left shoulder, or a pain in the stomach may be felt between the shoulder blades. Like other referred sensations, this **referred pain** is probably due to the way sense messages from the body are relayed up through the spinal cord to the brain. Sensory nerves that serve the skin may be linked to the same spinal relay nerve cells as the sensory nerves from internal body organs. The result is confusion about exactly where the pain message came from. Basically, there may sometimes be a "crossing of the wires."

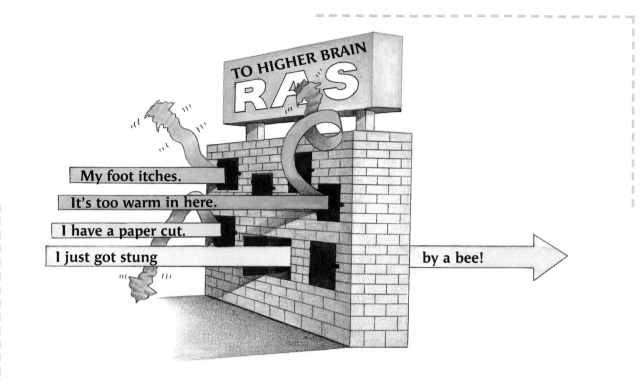

can make you yelp. Everybody has a different **pain threshold—** the weakest stimulus that is actually perceived as pain. Unless a stimulus is strong enough to reach this threshold, you will not feel any pain at all. Some people may react strongly to a mild stimulation of their pain receptors, while for others only a very strong stimulation of the pain receptors can cause noticeable pain. For instance, a skinned knee may not bother you very much, but the same kind of injury may cause your friend to cry out in agonizing pain.

The pain threshold can be raised when a person is distracted or concentrating on something else. A football player who injures his leg during an important game, for example, may hardly notice the pain until after the game, when the excitement is over. An engrossing book or movie may temporarily get rid of the nagging pain of a headache. How is it possible to ignore pain at certain times?

The answer is in the way the sense messages travel to the brain. Before the sense messages are processed in the higher brain, they pass through a region in the center of the brain called the **reticular** activating system (**RAS**). "Reticular" means netlike, and this part of the brain is a network of nerve fibers that acts as a clearinghouse. It screens the messages from the senses and sends on only those that seem interesting, unusual, or important. The more signals coming in, the more your mind tunes things out. That's why a football player will pay more attention to the exciting football game than to the pains in his leg. After the game, the incoming signals are greatly reduced, so the pain becomes more noticeable.

Minor aches and pains also seem to be more noticeable at night because the sense organs are not sending in as much other information. With less competition, the RAS sends these signals through to the higher brain.

NOT EXACTLY PAIN

Until recently, scientists believed that the sensations of tickling and itching both share the same nerve pathways as pain, although they are all considered to be distinct and separate sensations. It was thought that mild stimulation of the pain receptors produced a tickle, and a slightly stronger stimulation produced an itch. But then German and Swedish researchers discovered some special nerve fibers sensitive to itching. They are the smallest nerve cells found in humans, and they carry the slowest signals—about 1.6 feet (0.5 meter) per second, one-twentieth the speed that pain signals travel. Researchers have not yet found separate tickle receptors.

If somebody tries to tickle you, your body quickly reacts by jerking away to avoid further stimulation. But researchers still have not found separate tickle receptors.

Our immediate response to an itch is usually scratching. Scientists are not sure why scratching an itch makes it go away; it may be that scratching produces a new signal that either stops the spinal nerve vibrations or brings in a new sensation that competes

27

Strange Sensations

If you have ever had a tooth pulled, you know that the dentist will usually give you an anesthetic to numb your gums. Numbing is necessary to protect you from feeling pain, but at the same time, it gives you a very strange feeling. If your left hand has been injected with a local anesthetic, for example, and you touch it with your right hand, you can see yourself touching it, but you feel nothing with the numbed hand. It feels heavy and does not respond to any stimuli.

If your arm "goes to sleep" because you were resting your head on it, you feel a numbness and later a "pins and needles" feeling in your hand. What happened was that your head was pressing hard on the nerve endings in the skin, cutting off the sense messages to the brain. As the nerve signals return to normal when the pressure is removed, the numbness turns into a tingling "pins and needles" sensation, and finally you have normal sensations.

for attention. Various skin conditions and allergic reactions are known for causing itching.

Easing the Pain

Various drugs can be used to relieve pain. Aspirin, for example, works by stopping the production of chemicals that stimulate pain sensations. Morphine and other similar drugs stop the transmission of pain messages to the brain and spinal cord and may make a person feel good. Researchers have discovered that the body produces natural morphinelike painkillers, called **endorphins**. They think that people who can tolerate more pain than the average person may produce more endorphins. These chemicals are also produced during strenuous exercise.

Pain-relieving drugs are called **analgesics**. **Anesthetics** are drugs that block sensation in general. Local anesthetics injected near the site of an operation block the transmission of pain messages to the brain. This produces numbness—no feeling at all. General anesthesia, produced by drugs that are injected or inhaled, stops the perception of pain by causing unconsciousness.

It Takes Some Getting Used To

When a tactile stimulus continues for a while at the same strength, the receptors send fewer and fewer messages to the brain, and eventually you no longer feel it. This effect is called **adaptation**. Touch receptors adapt very quickly. This is a good thing. If your touch receptors were not able to adapt to continuing stimuli, you would never be able to wear

Some long-distance runners experience feelings of extreme happiness and well-being after about 20 minutes of running. This "runner's high" is believed to be due to the production of endorphins.

clothes. You would constantly have the feeling that something was pressing on you. Even the touch of the hair on your head would drive you crazy.

Pressure and pain receptors adapt much more slowly, and that is a good thing. Something that is pressing hard against your skin may cause damage, and something painful may already be damaging your body. Feelings of discomfort and pain are warning signals to prompt you to do something about a dangerous situation.

5 TEMPERATURE SENSES

If you look out your window, can you tell what the weather is? You can see that it is bright and sunny, and you deduce that the wind is blowing from the way the leaves are moving. But you probably can't tell if it is cold or warm outside. Unless you have an outdoor thermometer, the only way to find out what the temperature is outside is to go outside yourself. Your skin has special receptors that respond to warmth and cold. These temperature receptors, known as **thermoreceptors**, let you know if the weather is cold and you need to put a coat on or if it is warm enough to wear shorts.

Every day, we are exposed to varying temperatures, ranging from very cold to very hot. Our thermoreceptors are very sensitive to these changes in temperatures, and when exposure becomes uncomfortable or harmful, they prompt us to take some suitable action.

TEMPERATURE DETECTORS

The skin contains three different types of receptors that detect changes in temperature: **cold receptors**, **warmth receptors**, and **pain receptors**. The cold and warmth receptors work together with pain receptors to provide you with a built-in thermometer. You can tell just by feeling something whether it is hotter or colder than your body temperature, which is normally 98.6°F (37°C). The cold receptors, known as the **Krause end bulbs**, are activated when the skin comes into contact with temperatures colder than body temperature—from 54° to 95°F (12° to 35°C). Warmth receptors, called **Ruffini corpuscles**, are stimulated when exposed to higher temperatures, from 100° to 113°F (38° to 45°C). Pain receptors are stimulated only by temperatures that are very cold (below 54°F or 12°C) or very hot (above 113°F or 45°C). Touching something very hot or very cold produces just about the same sensation—pain. This can be really confusing to your brain, and you may not be able to tell the difference between very cold and very hot temperatures. That's why an ice cube may seem "burning hot."

Like the touch receptors, the thermoreceptors in your skin are also spread out all over the body, in varying numbers. The sensitive touch areas, however, are not necessarily the same as the sensitive temperature areas. The fingertips are important in touch but are far less sensitive to temperature than other parts of the body. That is why you can feel perfectly comfortable without gloves on a chilly fall day, but you need to wear a heavy sweater or jacket to feel warm. The tongue is also sensitive to touch, but it is not very sensitive to temperature. You can easily burn your tongue while eating a slice of hot pizza or drinking hot chocolate. But you may be able to avoid getting burned by testing the food or drink with a light touch of your lips. The lips and wrists are among the most sensitive regions for temperature. You get a more accurate result if you feel a person's forehead for a fever with your lips, rather than your hands.

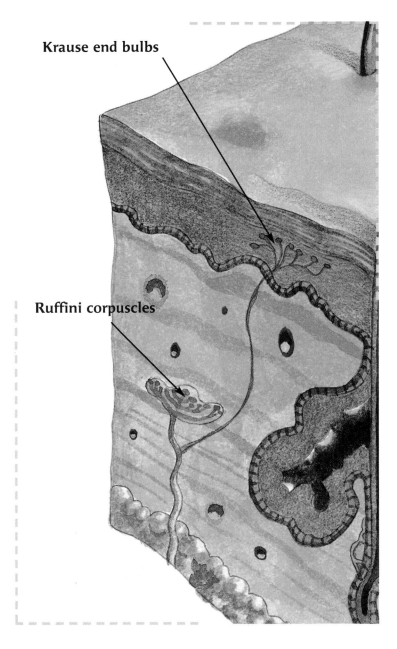

Krause end bulbs

Ruffini corpuscles

FOOLING THE BRAIN

Changes in temperature can sometimes confuse the brain. You can test this in an experiment. Place three bowls on the table: a bowl of hot water on the left, a bowl of cold water on the right, and a bowl of lukewarm water in the middle. Put your left hand in the hot water and your right hand in the cold water. After a few minutes, take both hands out and place them in the bowl of lukewarm water. Strangely, the two hands give different "temperature readings" for the same water. The lukewarm water feels cold to the left hand and hot to the right hand.

YOUR BODY'S THERMOSTAT

Just as you can turn up a thermostat in a room that feels cold, your body also has a kind of thermostat that is used to regulate temperature. Deep inside the brain, there is a tiny structure called the **hypothalamus**. It contains your body's temperature control center ("thermostat"). Whenever your body gets too cold or too warm, the hypothalamus sends nerve signals throughout the body to correct the problem.

When you start to feel cold, the tiny blood vessels close to the skin constrict (narrow). This allows less blood to flow through them, so less heat can escape out through the skin. Your body may also start shivering—the muscles start to move and shake to generate heat to warm you up.

In contrast, when you feel too warm, the tiny blood vessels widen, allowing more blood to flow close to the skin surface. Heat then radiates out from the surface of the body, helping to cool you down. You also respond to warm temperatures by sweating. The sweat glands become activated and release water from the sweat pores in the skin. The sweat absorbs heat from the skin's surface, which carries some of the heat away from the body. The water also evaporates, which gets rid of even more heat.

These kinds of reactions to temperature changes are reflex actions. They are automatic. You don't have to think about them. But you can also regulate your body temperature on a more conscious level. When you feel too cold, you can put on a heavy jacket or a coat to warm up. You can also keep warm through exercise. As in shivering, the motion of the muscles produces heat. If you are feeling too warm and you want to cool off, you can wear a T-shirt or tank top and shorts, have a cold drink, or go for a swim.

GETTING COMFORTABLE

Like the touch receptors, the thermoreceptors also have an amazing ability to adapt to stimuli. You probably know the feeling when you first step into a bathtub filled with hot water—*ouch!* It feels too hot to climb in right away, so you ease into the water slowly. After a few minutes, your thermoreceptors adapt, or get used to, the temperature change, and the water feels comfortable.

What happened was that the change in temperature strongly stimulated the thermoreceptors at first. With continued exposure, the warmth receptors quickly stop responding (although not completely), and the sensation is not as noticeable. The same thing happens when you first jump into a swimming pool that feels icy. The cold receptors soon stop being stimulated, and you get used to the pool water that you once considered very cold.

MORE ABOUT GOOSEBUMPS

We get goosebumps when it's cold mainly because we inherited this reaction from animal ancestors that had fur all over their bodies. For a furry animal, this is an effective reaction for staying warm. The raised hairs trap a thicker layer of air close to the body, which acts like an insulating blanket. This reflex doesn't work very well for humans, with our short, sparse body hair.

6 TOUCH SENSES IN ANIMALS

Our ancestors developed from single-celled creatures. We think of single-celled organisms as very simple forms of life, but actually they are aware of their surroundings and can respond to them in surprisingly complex ways. Their most basic sense is touch. If you are a single-celled organism floating in a pond, anything that touches you may be a threat or a potential source of food.

An amoeba, a pond-dweller that looks like no more than an animated blob of jelly, can sense touch, heat, cold, and various chemicals even though it has no organized sense organs. In fact, it somehow seems to "know" that other tiny water creatures can receive and respond to sense messages, too. If it is trying to eat a ciliate (an active swimming one-celled organism that could escape if it senses danger), it pushes out long **pseudopods**, armlike structures, that reach around its prey without touching it until it is completely surrounded. But if the same amoeba is eating an alga (a single-celled plantlike organism that cannot move away from danger), the amoeba just flows right up to and over it.

The paramecium, a single-celled organism that can swim, relies on its sense of touch to find its way through the water. If a paramecium bumps into something, like a weed or some algae, it will stop short. Then it will back away, turn slightly to one side, and try again. The paramecium will always turn the same amount and keep trying over and over until it finally finds a way out.

The hydra is a somewhat more complex animal. This pond-dweller is shaped like a vase with a ring of tentacles surrounding an

34

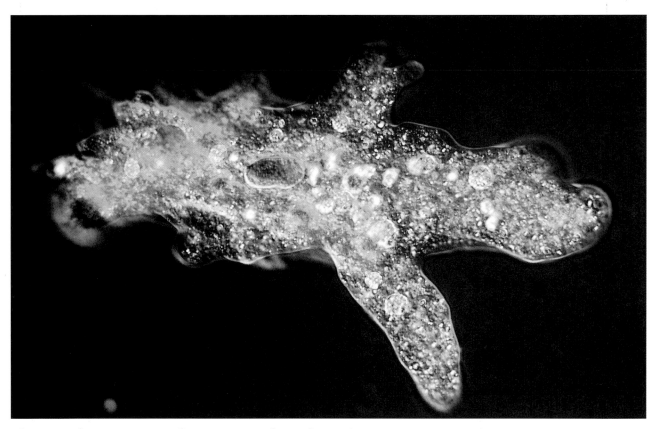

An amoeba can not only sense touch and varying temperatures, it can discern when other creatures have this ability too.

opening at the top. Its long, slim body is made up of many cells, specialized for different tasks. It has muscle cells that help to move its body; touch cells on its body surface that provide tactile information about its surroundings; thread cells that shoot out poison darts; and a simple net of nerves that coordinate its activities. The hydra spends most of its time attached to a plant or the mud at the bottom of the pond. It feeds on tiny water creatures that happen to float by. If one of them touches the hydra's tentacles, the thread cells shoot out poisonous threads that stun the prey and paralyze it. Then the hydra wraps its tentacles around its prey and draws the unlucky creature into its mouth. If something big touches a hydra, it sets off a different reflex. Muscle cells contract, shortening the hydra's body, and moving it away from the object that touched it.

As animals became more and more complex, their organs and systems became more complicated and highly developed. Among

The hydra has touch cells on its body that transmit tactile information about its environment. Here, the hydra is in the process of digesting a tiny water creature that foolishly touched the hydra's tentacles while floating by.

these changes, they developed special organs for tactile senses. These tactile senses vary a great deal, and some of them are more complex than others. Still, touch has many purposes in the animal kingdom: to locate food, navigate, find a mate, avoid danger, and communicate with others of their species.

ARTHROPODS

The simplest form of tactile senses can be found among the **invertebrates**, animals without backbones. One group of invertebrates are the **arthropods**, which include insects, spiders, scorpions, and crustaceans (such as crabs and lobsters). Most insects have tiny touch-sensitive hairs called **hair sensilla**, which are scattered all over their bodies. The sensilla contain many highly sensitive touch receptors, which can detect vibrations on the ground, in the water, and through the air. The sensilla on a butterfly's wings feel the air currents and help it to catch the breezes that let it fly.

Some insects, such as ants, crickets, and cockroaches, use their long antennae, or "feelers," as organs of touch. The antennae are covered with sensilla. An ant uses its antennae to collect information about food. By touching a morsel with its antennae, it can get an idea of its shape and size. If the object is too large to carry, the ant will get help to break it up into smaller, more manageable pieces. The ant also uses its antennae to touch the ground so it can feel its way home.

The praying mantis, which has hundreds of sensilla all over its body, depends on its sense of touch for hunting. The mantis frequently moves its head, which is covered with sensilla, to detect approaching prey. The touch-sensitive

The housefly has hair sensilla all over its body. These contain many sensitive touch receptors that can detect vibrations, such as when a threatening enemy is about to attack.

hairs are so effective that the praying mantis knows the location of the victim and exactly how far it is. It can then attack with great accuracy.

A scorpion, the insect's distant relative, cannot see, hear, or smell to find its prey. Instead, it relies on its sense of touch. When a scorpion hunts, the sensilla on its eight legs can detect the vibrations of a moving insect in the desert sand. The scorpion locates the insect by following the vibrations. It then darts over to the victim, grabs it with its **pedipalps** (pincers), and then paralyzes it with the poisonous sting at the end of its tail.

Here, a trap-door spider lifts the lid of its trap and emerges from its hideout.

The scorpion's web-spinning cousin, the spider, also uses its sense of touch to detect prey. When an insect flies into a spider's sticky web, it gets stuck and struggles to get free. The spider can feel the silky threads vibrate under its feet, and it follows the vibrations until it finds its unlucky victim. The spider can also tell how big or small the prey is by the strength of the vibrations. A mild vibration may indicate the presence of a small, helpless victim, which the spider can easily overpower and kill. But a stronger, more vigorous vibration may mean the prey is big and possibly dangerous, and the spider approaches with caution. Hunting by touch also allows the spider to hunt at night as well as during the day.

Not all spiders weave webs, but they still hunt by touch. One kind of trap-door spider, for example, lives in a hole in the ground, which is covered with a hinged lid made out of the spider's silky thread. At night, the spider stretches its legs out of the trapdoor opening. Its legs are covered with sensilla. When an insect brushes against the touch-sensitive hairs, the spider, anchored to its home with its back legs, grabs the insect and drags it into the burrow to be eaten.

Another kind of trap-door spider covers its burrow opening with a leaf. When an insect moves across the leaf, the leaf vibrates. The spider feels the vibrations with its touch-sensitive hairs and then rushes out of the burrow to grab its meal. Still another kind of trap-door spider spins silky "trip wires" over its burrow opening. When an insect trips over these threads, the spider feels the vibrating thread and quickly races out to attack its prey.

Crustaceans, such as lobsters and crabs, rely on their sense of touch to locate food, detect danger, find mates, and avoid obstacles. They have touch-sensitive bristles and hairs all over the body, and on the legs and antennae. They can detect vibrations in the sand and in water. The hairs on a crab's claws can also tell how hard or soft an object is.

REPTILES

Many reptiles depend on their sense of touch for survival. Reptiles are cold-blooded animals, which means that they cannot maintain their body temperature. So they rely on the sun to warm their bodies. Reptiles have touch receptors beneath their tough, leathery scales. These touch receptors are very sensitive to temperature. Their sensors let them know when they need sun to warm up or shade to cool down.

Female iguanas check the temperature of the sand before they begin to lay their eggs. Unless it is close to 86°F (30°C), the eggs will not hatch. The iguana can feel the sand's temperature with receptors under its skin.

A clear glass windowpane probably feels smooth to your fingertips, but a gecko's sensitive touch can actually feel the tiny grooves and ridges on its surface. A gecko can climb up a window

PLANTS CAN TOUCH TOO

Twining vines "feel their way" as they twist around tree trunks and even up the sides of houses. Carnivorous, or meat-eating, plants live mainly by touch. They have touch-sensitive leaves that snap shut when they are touched. When an insect lands on the outstretched leaves of a Venus's-flytrap, for example, the plant feels the insect's vibrating movements, and quickly closes its leaves to trap its prey.

or scurry across the ceiling without falling because its feet have tiny hooks, which grab onto the rough surface like Velcro.

Crocodiles have many touch receptors underneath their scales, mostly on their heads and necks. Like other reptiles, they are very sensitive to hot and cold temperatures. They often stay in the water at night because water holds in the heat longer than air does. Crocodiles also use their sensitive touch as a form of communication with other crocodiles. They rub necks and snouts with those of other crocodiles, especially during the mating season.

Snakes can gather information about their surroundings by feeling vibrations in the ground through their bodies. They can feel a person's footsteps from many yards away or sense a tiny mouse scurrying through the grass. The strong vibrations of a person's footsteps are likely to scare the snake away. But the light vibrations made by the little mouse may draw the snake closer to investigate.

BIRDS

Touch is important to certain species of birds, as well. The mallard duck, for example, has many touch receptors, mostly inside its bill and on its webbed feet. The mallard uses its sensitive bill to search for food in the murky waters and muddy bottoms of lakes and rivers.

A mallard's webbed feet are also very sensitive to touch. Ducks are careful when they walk on the ground, avoiding sharp sticks and rocks that may hurt their feet.

MAMMALS

People love to touch cats because their soft fur feels good to us. Cats love to be petted because the gentle touch feels good to them. Even though a cat's body is covered with thick fur, it is very sensitive to touch. Many of a cat's hairs are connected directly into touch receptor cells. Like people, a cat has more touch receptors in some areas than others, as well as different kinds of touch receptors. The pads on a cat's paws and the hairs between them are very sensitive to touch. If you lightly touch these places, you'll notice that the cat may quickly try to pull its paws away.

A cat's whiskers, known as **vibrissae**, have touch receptors in the hair roots and hair follicles. The slightest touch on a whisker

The touch receptors on the mole's snout detect vibrations
that inform the mole if there is a tasty meal ahead
or the possibility of danger.

sends messages to the cat's brain. A cat's whiskers can detect vibrations of anything moving nearby, even a tiny mouse. When a cat catches a mouse, its whiskers curl around its prey to keep track of its squirming movements. The whiskers can also be used as a navigating device. A cat can easily "feel" its way around a pitch-black room with its whiskers and avoid bumping into walls and objects.

Moles depend greatly on their sense of touch. They live in dark, underground burrows and spend a lot of time digging tunnels. They are practically blind and use their sense of touch to find their way. The mole has thousands of whiskerlike touch receptors in the vibrissae on its pink snout. These touch receptors can detect vibrations of any moving objects. The mole's short tail is also covered with sensory hairs. As the mole travels through the tunnels, it often brushes its tail against the walls and roof of the burrow to detect any vibrations.

7 THE IMPORTANCE OF TOUCH

Before you were born, you were constantly "in touch" with your mother. Her body surrounded you. You felt her every movement, and she could feel when you kicked or turned inside her belly. As you grew inside your mother, you felt warm and secure.

Touch is still an important part of our lives even after birth. We often use our sense of touch to connect with other people—our family, friends, and even strangers. We can learn a lot about the people we interact with through their touch and interpret many different meanings from these experiences.

COMMUNICATING THROUGH TOUCH

A little boy gives his mother a hug when she goes off to work. Two friends give each other high fives when they see each other at school. A businessman shakes his client's hand when they meet for their appointment. Baseball players run together for a group hug after winning a big game. Every day, we communicate with each other not just through speaking and listening, but through our touch as well.

People often use touch to express their feelings. You may give your aunt a big hug after she gives you a really neat gift for your birthday. Or maybe you hug your dad after he changes his mind and says that you can go out to the movies with your friends. If you fall off your bike and hurt your knee, you may need a comforting hug from your mom. Or you may need a hug if you did badly on a test. Getting a hug or some other comforting touch makes us feel good.

People are so aware of the benefits of touching that we often say "I need a hug" when we are feeling down or depressed.

STARVING FOR TOUCH

Touch is the only sense we literally cannot live without. People who are blind or deaf can learn to heighten their other senses. Those who lose the ability to smell or taste may lose some of the pleasures in life, but can somehow manage. But a person who does not get the right amount of touching can die.

Scientists say that people who don't get enough touch in their lives have a "skin hunger." This can be compared to the kind of hunger you feel when you haven't eaten for a while. You feel starved for food. Similarly, you have skin hunger when your skin is starved—for touch.

Studies show that babies who are touched often are much healthier than those who are not. In fact, it is possible for children to become malnourished and even die if they are not receiving an adequate amount of touching.

When a child is born, the mother's first bond with her infant is through touching. Babies not only want to be touched, they *need* it. Scientists had to discover the importance of touching the hard way.

During the first half of the twentieth century, there was a widespread belief that children who were given too much attention and handled too often became spoiled and unruly. Mothers were told that they should just let their babies "cry it out" and keep them on a strict schedule dictating when to eat and when to sleep. After some time, doctors noticed a sharp increase in deaths among "healthy" babies at a number of orphanages and hospitals. There was no explanation for the deaths. The children basically became withdrawn, lost weight, and died. Doctors later discovered that these children died because they were starving for touch.

Since then, many studies have been conducted on the importance of touch. Some of the findings showed that premature babies whose mothers massaged, rocked, and talked to them regularly gained weight and left the hospital sooner than those who did not receive such attention.

Researchers have also conducted studies with monkeys. They took newborn rhesus monkeys from their mothers and introduced them to two devices that acted as mothers. Both devices provided the baby monkeys with milk. One "mother," however, was made out of wire, while the other was made of soft padding. The monkeys preferred to go to the padded mother, constantly clinging to it and hugging it. When the monkeys were frightened, they immediately ran to the padded mother. In another experiment, the baby monkeys were allowed to have only one surrogate mother. The monkeys with a wire mother became depressed, withdrawn, and confused. The group with the padded mother were carefree and played happily.

Studies have continued to show that touch is not only essential to a child's physical well-being but also helps a child to develop intellectually and emotionally. Touching stimulates brain activity, allowing the formation of important neural (nerve) connections.

PERSONAL TOUCH

People in some cultures do not touch as much as those in other cultures. In the United States, many people like to have a significant amount of "personal space." When two people speak to each other, for example, there must be room between them so they can feel comfortable. When the personal space is invaded, a person may become uncomfortable or upset, and have trouble concentrating on the conversation. In some countries, such as Turkey, Italy, and India, the personal space is much smaller. People feel comfortable and natural standing close to one another. In fact, soldiers in these countries can be seen holding hands or walking arm in arm.

Your personal space is determined by the country in which you live; it may also be determined by the home and family in which you grow up. A warm, close upbringing may lessen your personal space, whereas a cooler, more distant upbringing may widen your personal space.

Therefore, children who are held often are much more responsive to intellectual stimuli than those who are not. In addition, children who do not receive adequate touching are less likely to form trusting or loving relationships in adulthood.

TOUCH THERAPY

Since prehistoric times, people have had the idea that the "laying on of hands"—touching—can not only make people feel better in general, but can even heal illnesses. Paintings in caves in the Pyrenees mountains between France and Spain dating from about 15,000 years ago show people healing by touch. The touching technique is shown in records from ancient China, Egypt, and Thailand, and the "hands-on" healing powers of Jesus are mentioned many times in the New Testament.

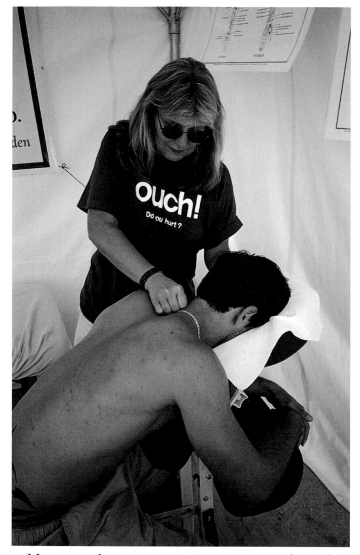

Massage therapy can serve emotional needs while healing a variety of physical ailments.

Today, various methods of **massage**—rubbing, kneading, or patting the body—are used to bring relief from pain and to help heal muscle strains and relieve tension. Some people believe that massage can actually help to heal diseases that affect the body's internal organs. The massage stimulates circulation, and the increased blood flow brings oxygen, nutrients, and other chemicals that help the body to repair damaged tissues. In fact, the natural impulse to "rub the place that hurts" is an instinct that helps us tap these healing powers.

Although touch therapy has been around for thousands of years, it wasn't until recently that it started to get widespread recognition in the United States. In 1993, an article published by

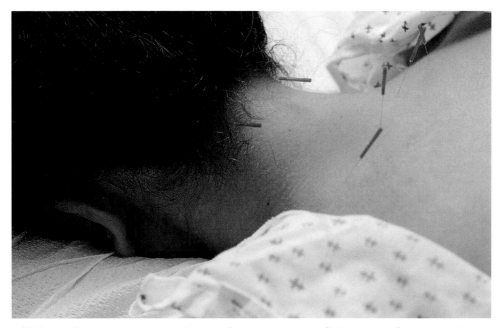

Although acupuncture is used to treat conditions such as anxiety, arthritis, eczema, asthma, migraines, and high blood pressure, the ultimate goal is to restore the individual's physical, emotional, and spiritual balance.

The New England Journal of Medicine reported a study that found that one-third of the United States population was using alternative medicine, involving methods that doctors considered to be unconventional. The most popular method of alternative medicine was touch therapy. This landmark article paved the way for touch therapy, allowing it to be embraced by the medical community as a legitimate form of treatment.

Over the years, various forms of massage have been introduced to the United States from all over the world. Probably the most popular method is Swedish massage. Swedish massage is best known for its deep relaxation techniques. But studies have shown that it also helps people's physical well-being: it can relieve pain, ease nausea, boost the immune system, and help premature infants gain weight.

Chinese medicine has been another important influence in touch therapy. The Chinese wrote about massage in medical treatment as early as 4,000 years ago. Most people are probably familiar

DID YOU KNOW?

Hands-on healing used to be a big part of the family doctor's treatments, but busy modern doctors usually rely on prescription drugs and leave the hands-on practices to nurses and physical therapists.

Did You Know?

Touching has a calming effect: It reduces aggression, tension, and anxiety.

with acupuncture, an ancient Chinese technique in which needles are inserted in certain points on a person's body. The acupuncture points stimulate the flow of a person's *chi*—the life force that exists in all living things. A similar technique, called acupressure, works on the same principle but is much simpler to perform because it does not involve needles. Generally, the therapist uses fingers, thumbs, or knuckles to place pressure on certain points on the body. These techniques are very helpful in relaxing the body and relieving pain and nausea.

8
TOUCH TECHNOLOGY

When you go to sleep at night, what kind of dreams do you have? Maybe you can fly around the world like Superman, or you're a rock star in a music video. Perhaps you dream about being on a fantasy date. Whenever you dream, you live in a virtual world. Dreams are more than just pictures that we paint in our minds. Dreams feel real to us. We can actually interact with the people, places, and objects in our dreams. It's kind of like being in a three-dimensional movie. You can feel the hard, pointy corners of a table, the painful impact when you get hit by a ball, or the soft, enjoyable feeling of a kiss.

Computer scientists have created a way to turn dreams into a "virtual reality" through computer technology called **virtual reality** (VR). Virtual reality is a simulation of an environment, created with computer hardware and software, and presented to the user so that it looks and feels like the "real thing." Virtual reality is best known for its entertainment uses, but it also has many practical applications.

Scientists have also been working hard on a variety of other projects that utilize the sense of touch. Today, touch sensors are widely used in computer systems. Just a click of the mouse involves touch sensing. Some computer screens are also sensitive to the light touch of a human finger. "Robot hands" equipped with touch sensors have also been devised to help humans investigate dangerous or inaccessible areas. Scientists use the term **haptic** for touch senses and devices that use touch senses to guide actions.

A Virtual World

If you want to go on a virtual reality adventure, you must wear special goggles or a helmet hooked up to a computer. The computer transmits images to two tiny video screens in the headgear, one for each eye. The images are slightly different for each eye, which makes the image appear real, lifelike, and three-dimensional.

Sensors in the equipment may allow you to interact with the virtual world. Haptic sensors detect your movements and report them to the computer. The computer then makes adjustments in response to your actions. For instance, if you turn your head, the scene changes. Some VR systems involve a special glove, which tracks the hand movements. Other systems have joysticks like those used in video games. And some systems use treadmill devices so you can walk through the virtual world. There is even a special suit that reports body movements. Although virtual reality is an amazing technology, computer experts say the images are not completely realistic. But they expect a much better virtual-reality experience as

An urban planner uses a virtual reality system to visualize how proposed roadwork will affect local traffic patterns. The headset allows him to obtain different views by turning his head, and the glove can be used to highlight specific objects on the screen.

50

imaging technology continues to develop in the coming years.

Virtual reality is not just used for entertainment. VR is used in medical training, for instance. Doctors in training can practice surgical techniques on virtual patients while being directed by the computer. Holding a forceps in one hand and a needle holder in the other while watching the monitor screen, for example, apprentice surgeons can practice grasping a slippery blood vessel and sewing it to another one. Haptic feedback gives them the feel of an actual needle popping through the vessel wall and lets them know how tightly they are pulling. And if trainee doctors make mistakes, they don't risk the lives of any real patients.

TOUCH AND GO

Touch plays an important role in using a computer, whether you're writing a report, playing games, or surfing the net. The computer mouse, a popular tracking device, is equipped with specialized touch and pressure sensors. Sensors in the mouse track its movements on the mousepad, which are translated into electrical signals that determine the path of the cursor moving across the screen. When you click on an item on the screen, pressure sensors in the mouse buttons detect the pressure of your fingertip and send signals to the computer that command it to open a menu, answer a question, go to a new Web page, or perform some other action.

Another pointing device, the trackball, is simply a mouse turned upside down. The touch of your finger rolling the ball guides the cursor. Touchpads have touch and pressure sensors under a small sensitive surface. You can trace a path with a light touch of your fingertip or give a harder tap to "click" a button. In some computers, such as those found in banks or malls, the whole screen

AN EMOTIONAL MOUƧE

Research is underway on a computer mouse designed to evaluate a person's emotional state. This electronic device contains pressure sensors that respond to every click. It measures pulse, temperature, and the skin's ability to conduct electricity (which indicates how much the hands are perspiring). Studies have shown a definite link between physical signs and emotions. Anger results in an increased heart rate, high muscle tension, and deep breathing. Grief brings slower, shallow breathing and a reduced electric conductivity of the skin.

This boy is using a brain-activated system to play a computer game with his friend, while she uses a standard mouse. A sensor on the boy's finger monitors his mental activity by measuring his heartbeat, temperature, pulse, and electrical signals in his skin. A computer program filters out unconscious nerve impulses and only responds to the conscious signals.

is a sensitive touchpad. With a light press of your finger you can interact with the computer program to answer questions, perform banking transactions, find your way around a mall, or even go shopping.

The latest pointing device, the "iFeel MouseMan," introduced in 2000, provides touch feedback to involve the user more fully in the computer experience. When the mouse moves over an icon or a specially programmed link on a Web page, a vibrating device inside the mouse gives the user a touch signal. The icon may emit a rubbery or metallic feel, a reverberating "sonicvibe," or the sensation of a bouncy basketball, depending on how the user has programmed it. Using the new technology, Web sites can allow shoppers to feel the material of clothing or furniture. But this new mouse has eliminated another aspect of touch in its operation: Instead of a rolling ball that senses movement, it uses a beam of light to track its position.

ROBOT HANDS

Since the 1980s, scientists have been getting closer to duplicating many of the human senses, including the sense of touch, for use in artificial devices—robots—to substitute for humans in various tasks. Some are human- or animal-like machines that can move around independently; others are just the working parts needed for particular tasks, such as a robot arm that has tactile sensors and is designed to work like a human hand. These robot hands have mechanical fingers, which can grasp and manipulate objects. Haptic sensors provide information about the shape and size of the object, which is used as feedback to guide the robot's actions. Robots are now being used in manufacturing plants, on outer space missions, to recover wreckage under water, and to perform difficult tasks in dangerous environments that are too risky for humans. Researchers are also developing a robotic hand that can spell out the letters of words on the palm of a deaf-blind person's hand. People can communicate with the user over a telephone line, typing on a computer keyboard that transmits signals to control the robot hand.

Haptic sensors are also being used to develop more realistic and useful **prosthetics**, mechanical replacements for lost hands, arms, or legs. The developers of the first "bionic" hands and feet focused mainly on the movements such devices must perform and the miniaturized motors and computer-chip "brains" to guide them. They soon realized, however, that a feedback of sensory information was just as important. When you pick up an egg, for example, you have to use just enough force to hold it securely—and no more. If you feel it start to slip, you automatically tighten your grip, but not so much that you would crack the eggshell. Today's haptic devices can provide this feedback information for prosthetic

A deaf and blind girl tests a robot hand that spells words into her hand with its fingers. Yet, she immediately discovers a problem. The robot hand shifts into neutral between each letter, creating unnatural delays.

hands, using various ways to transmit the sense impressions to the brain. Similarly, prosthetic feet with pressure sensors in their soles and other haptic sensors in their joints allow users to track the movements of the feet while walking and know when they are standing with their weight evenly distributed between the two feet. Researchers are also developing prosthetic limbs that can be connected directly to a person's sensory and motor nerves, allowing sense messages and action commands to be transmitted along the same pathways used by the original limbs.

Along the way to developing sophisticated new devices for touch technology, researchers are learning more about how our own tactile senses work. The insights they are gaining can help to enrich our world and increase our enjoyment of all the experiences it offers.

This android robot named Cog was developed to help us learn how having a body influences artificial intelligence. Its visual system guides the movements of its hand, which has a touch-sensitive surface that allows the robot to classify the objects it is holding, adjust its grip accordingly, and tell when the object is slipping.

GLOSSARY

adaptation—a decrease in the response of sensory receptors to a stimulus that continues for an extended time

analgesics—pain-relieving drugs

anesthetics—drugs that block sensations in general

arthropods—a group of invertebrates that includes insects, spiders, scorpions, and crustaceans (such as crabs and lobsters)

central nervous system (CNS)—the part of the nervous system that consists of the brain and spinal cord

cerebral cortex—the thin, outermost layer of the brain where most of the activity in the brain takes place; *see* cerebrum

cerebrum—the largest part of the brain, with which we think, remember, process sensory information, make decisions, and control the movements of the body

cold receptors—thermoreceptors that respond to cold temperatures

corpus callosum—a thick cable of nerve fibers deep inside the brain that links the two brain hemispheres and permits an exchange of information between them

endorphins—natural painkillers produced in the body

free nerve endings—nerve endings that are stimulated by objects that lightly touch the skin

hair end-organs—sense receptors found in hairy parts of the body that respond to light moving touches through the hairs

hair sensilla—touch-sensitive hairs

haptic—tactile; pertaining to touch sense and its use as feedback for adjusting and controlling actions in interactive devices

hemispheres—two halves of the brain, the left and the right

hypothalamus—a structure deep inside the brain that contains a number of control centers, including the one that controls body temperature

invertebrates—animals without backbones or an internal skeleton

Krause end bulbs—cold receptors

massage—a method of rubbing, kneading, or patting the body, designed to bring relief from pain and to help heal muscle strains and relieve tension

Meissner's corpuscles—sense receptors found in the lips, fingertips, and other sensitive places that respond to very light touch

Merkel's disks—sense receptors found mostly on the tongue and in hairy parts of the body. They detect continuous touch of objects against the skin.

motor nerves—nerves that carry messages from the CNS to the muscles and other organs and produce actions, many of which are movements

motor strip—portion of the cerebral cortex from which messages are sent out to the various parts of the body to direct movements

neurons—nerve cells

Pacinian corpuscles—onion-shaped receptors found all over in the skin, connective tissue near tendons and joints, and various deep tissues. They are very sensitive to pressure and vibrations.

pain receptors—thermoreceptors that respond to extreme temperatures, chemicals, and other potentially damaging stimuli

pain threshold—the weakest stimulus that is actually perceived as pain

pedipalps—in arachnids, a pair of legs specially modified for sensory functions

prosthetics—mechanical replacements for lost hands, arms, or legs

pseudopods—armlike structures in single-celled creatures, such as the amoeba

referred pain—painful sensation felt in a different place from the body part that is actually being hurt, due to confusion in the brain's processing of incoming messages from the branching network of sensory nerves

referred sensation—sensation felt in a different place from where it actually originated, due to confusion in the brain's processing of incoming messages from the branching network of sensory nerves

reflex—automatic reaction to a stimulus, directed by the spinal cord rather than the brain

reticular activating system (RAS)—a network of nerve fibers in the brain that screens incoming messages from the senses and sends on only those that seem unusual, interesting, or important

Ruffini corpuscles—warmth receptors

Ruffini's end-organs—multibranched nerve endings that respond to pressure and heavy continuous touch stimuli

sensors—specialized structures that gather information about the world. They detect various types of energy and transmit signals to the brain.

sensory cortex—an area of the brain where sensory messages are interpreted and we become aware of touching and of other senses

sensory nerves—nerves that bring sense messages to the brain and spinal cord

sensory strip—a strip of cerebral cortex (just behind a groove that runs down each side of the brain, above the ears) where sense messages are processed

somesthetic areas—the sensory strip

tactile—touch

thalamus—a relay station in the brain that receives sensory messages

thermoreceptors—temperature receptors that respond to cold, warmth, or extreme temperatures

vibration—a series of rapid, repeated touches

vibrissae—sensory hairs at the sides of the mouth in some animals, as in the whiskers of a cat

virtual reality—a simulation of an environment, created with computer hardware and software, and presented to the user so that it looks and feels like the "real thing"

warmth receptors—thermoreceptors that respond to heat

FURTHER READING

Barré, Michel. *Animal Senses.* Milwaukee: Gareth Stevens Publishing, 1998.

Cobb, Vicki. *How to Really Fool Yourself: Illusions for All Your Senses.* New York: John Wiley & Sons, Inc., 1999.

Hellman, Hal. *Beyond Your Senses: The New World of Sensors.* New York: Lodestar Books, 1997.

Hickman, Pamela. *Animal Senses: How Animals See, Hear, Taste, Smell, and Feel.* Buffalo: Kids Can Press Ltd., 1998.

Llamas, Andreu. *The Five Senses of the Animal World: Touch.* New York: Chelsea House Publishers, 1996.

Parker, Steve. *Look at Your Body: Senses.* Brookfield, CT: Copper Beech Books, 1997.

Santa Fe Writers Group. *Bizarre & Beautiful Feelers.* Santa Fe: John Muir Publications, 1993.

Sullivan, Karin Horgan. *The Healing Power of Touch.* Lincolnwood, IL: Publications International, Ltd., 1998.

INTERNET RESOURCES

sln.fi.edu/qa97/me10/me10.html

"Minutes from Me: Touching," The Franklin Institute Online.

tqjunior.advanced.org/3750/index.html

"Come to Your Senses."

www.bae.ncsu.edu/bae/research/blanchard/www/465/textbook/otherprojects/
   senses_97/nevill/tactile.html

"The General Senses."

www.hhmi.org/senses

"Seeing, Hearing, and Smelling the World: New Findings Help Scientists Make
   Sense of Our Senses," The Howard Hughes Medical Institute.

INDEX